CW01019345

VERBAL REASONING

TECHNIQUE AND PRACTICE 1

Susan J. Daughtrey M.Ed

Childs World Education Limited
1993

ACKNOWLEDGEMENTS

I would like to thank my husband Brian without whose patient support and encouragement this series of books would not have been written. I must also express my thanks to our children Sara and James who enthusiastically contributed many ideas and performed numerous practical exercises. And finally, a special thanks to my students who (often unknowingly) provided the inspiration and feedback which has been so encouraging.

Brancaster, Norfolk.
1993.

ISBN 1 898696 46 2

Childs World Education Limited
PO Box 1881, Gerrards Cross,
Buckinghamshire SL9 9AN England

Printed in Great Britain by Halstan & Co. Ltd., Amersham, Bucks.

First published 1993.
First edition 1993.
Reprinted 1994 (twice), 1995, 1996, 1997, 1998 (twice), 2001.
Revised 2001.

TECHNIQUE TYPE ONE

Here you are simply required to identify TWO words which have changed places with each other. These deliberately misplaced words must be identified and by rearranging the two words in your head, a sensible sentence can be made. You must underline the two words to gain one mark. All other words must remain in the same order.

Example:

Play went outside to *Sarah*.

Here, *play* and *Sarah* have swopped places, so *play* and *Sarah* should be underlined. The sentence should read:

Sarah went outside to play.

Technique:

1.   Read the sentence quickly.

2.   Look up.   (Take your eyes off the words.)

3.   Think: What is this sentence trying to say?

4.   Decide on the answer. (If possible without looking back at the sentence.)

5.   Look back and mentally make the sentence say it.
     Underline the misplaced words.

6.   Reread the sentence with the misplaced words you have underlined, mentally corrected.

7.   Check the sentence does make sense.

NOTE:

1. Once you have discovered the first of the two words which is out of place, this will automatically change places with the word which should go in its place. In the above example, once you realise *play* is out of order and that it should read 'Sarah went.....' then Sarah must automatically be the other word which is out of place. In other words it is really only necessary to discover the first word which is wrongly placed. The second word should then automatically present itself.

2. Occasionally the uncorrected sentence has been written so two identical words, such as *the* and *the*, have been deliberately placed next to each other. If it is necessary to underline one of the words 'the', be sure to underline the correct

the. For this reason it is VERY important you always check your answer makes complete sense.

Example:

> The cat sat on the mat,   may be rewritten
> On cat sat the the mat.

Which *the* should be underlined?
The first one.
To underline any 'the' without checking is careless and may cost you a mark.
Take care!

3. Occasionally, also, two adjacent words (words next to each other) have changed places. This sometimes makes it more difficult to see. Read the sentence slowly and carefully and reread it if necessary before looking up and deciding what the sentence should say.

Example: Answers:

What time it is?	*is*	*it*
How it is you came first?	*is*	*it*
When you are coming to my house?	*are*	*you*
Is now the time for celebration.	*now*	*is*

4. Look carefully to see if the sentence asks a question. Is there a question mark at the end of the sentence? If it is meant to, make it. If it does not have a question mark, it does not ask a question. It is a statement. Make sure then it states a fact.

Example:

> *It is* a cold day?   should be corrected to read
> Is it a cold day?
> as there is a question mark at the end of the sentence.

> *Is milk* good for you.   should be corrected to read
> Milk is good for you.
> as there is a full stop at the end of the sentence. It states a fact.

You are allowed 30 seconds per question.

Now turn to the next page for Practice of this Type.

PRACTICE TYPE ONE

Underline the TWO words which should change places with each other in order to make sense of the following sentences.

For Example:

He put a <u>desk</u> on his <u>book</u>.

Now try these:

The boy kicked the the into ball net.

The dog lay next his to basket.

The rabbit scampers into the field and across its burrow.

Quickly car sped the along the motorway.

The fireman climbed down the tree to bring up the cat.

The cold fire warmed up the hot room.

Boy Scouts enjoy sleeping in out the open air.

She took her scarf out of the drawer and put into it her bag.

Milk is good for you ?

Put the table under the slippers.

Please quiet be in the library !

Deck standing on the top no of the bus.

No eating church in !

Take your cloakroom out of the shoes.

Thirty nine and forty two make seventy seven.

If tomorrow is Friday yesterday was Sunday.

Suddenly the lights went in out the theatre.

She looked herself at in the mirror.

Do not in come through the window !

The bend trees fir in the wind.

TECHNIQUE TYPE TWO

In these questions you are looking for a SIMILAR connection between two sets of facts. Once identified, you must underline the correct relationship to gain one mark.

Example:

> BIRD is to (egg, nest, feathers) as CAT is to (mice, fur, tail)

Technique:

1.   Ask: in what way can BIRD be related to each of the three features in the brackets?

> Answer: Birds lay eggs.
> A bird lives in a nest.
> Birds are covered with feathers.

2.   Similarly, ask: in what way can CAT be related to each of its three features given in brackets ?

> Answer: Cats chase mice.
> Cats are covered with fur.
> A cat has a tail.

3.   You are looking for a SIMILAR connection between BIRD and one of its features, and CAT and one of its features. That we are talking about both animals being 'covered' with something is the connection.

The correct answer here is:

> BIRD is to (egg, nest, *feathers*) as CAT is to (mice, *fur*, tail)

Example:

> TENNIS is to (court, net, racket) as CRICKET is to (summer, bat, pads)

1.   Here:
Tennis is played on a court.
Tennis needs a net.
Tennis is played with a racket.

2.   Similarly:
Cricket is played in summer.
Cricket is played with a bat.
The batsman wears pads.

The SIMILAR connection here must be the equipment used to hit the ball, the racket and the bat. So, the answer is:

> TENNIS is to (court, net, *racket*) as CRICKET is to (summer, *bat*, pads)

Example:

HAT is to (*head*, helmet, protection) as SHOE is to (*foot*, lace, buckle)

Here it is obvious that HAT is to *head*, as SHOE is to *foot*. While each of the features in brackets is in some way connected to the word outside the brackets, 'where the item is worn' is the only SIMILAR connection in both sets.

NOTE:

1. Sometimes it is a spelling relationship - that is, the word in brackets is a spelling alteration of the word outside the brackets. The same spelling alteration is made to both words - hence the connection.

Example:

BAND is to (elastic, *brand*, music) as CAMP is to (tent, field, *cramp*)

Here, an *r* has been inserted into both of the words to give *brand* and *cramp*. This is the only connection. Similarly:

PAST is to (verb, history, *passed*) as MIST is to (fog, cloud, *missed*)

Each simply has another spelling of

PAST	=	*passed*
MIST	=	*missed*

Take care!

2. Look particularly in number or time questions for another number or time to be involved:

THREE is to (*6*, 30, trio) as FIVE is to (*8*, fingers, 25)

Here, *6* and *8* are the correct answers - both have had three added. There is no similar relationship in the remaining features.

3. Sometimes a word can be spelled backwards. For example:

DOOM is to (end, *mood*, fate) as MEET is to (greet, kiss, *teem*)

Here,	DOOM	=	*mood*
	MEET	=	*teem*

You are allowed 30 seconds per question.

Now turn to the next page for Practice of this Type.

PRACTICE TYPE TWO

In each of the following, there is the SAME connection between the word outside each set of brackets and one word inside each set of brackets. You must find this same connection and then underline the TWO words, one from each set of brackets.

For Example:

Dog is to (paw, *meat*, tail) as cow is to (milk, calf, *grass*)

Now try these:

Car is to (road, wheel, garage) as barge is to (coal, lock, canal)

Hat is to (head, sun, brim) as hand is to (fingers, glove, wrist)

Finger is to (digit, ring, nail) as wrist is to (bracelet, arm, joint)

Doom is to (end, fate, mood) as room is to (door, moor, box)

Flame is to (heat, glow, red) as bulb is to (lamp, glass, light)

Daffodil is to (bulb, spring, yellow) as strawberry is to (red, sweet, cream)

Evil is to (wicked, bad, live) as emit is to (exit, time, eject)

Tree is to (branch, root, leaf) as house is to (dwelling, door, foundations)

Tick is to (trick, correct, good) as pick is to (flower, prick, stitch)

Author is to (book, picture, print) as music is to (note, composer, lively)

5 is to (10, 25, fingers) as 20 is to (25, 150, score)

Millimetre is to (ruler, metre, line) as litre is to (liquid, millilitre, bottle)

Cat is to (fur, tail, cart) as pat is to (part, stroke, pet)

Summer is to (fun, holiday, hot) as winter is to (snowman, dark, cold)

Fruit is to (tree, apple, bowl) as vegetable is to (potato, pie, meat)

Pencil is to (paper, pen, lead) as pen is to (ink, feather, write)

Rectangle is to (pentagon, cuboid, four) as triangle is to (angle, base, rectangle)

Television is to (look, set, colour) as radio is to (music, sound, listen)

Water is to (rain, steam, stream) as liquid is to (gas, flow, solid)

Pencil is to (pen, write, paper) as brush is to (paint, picture, palette)

TECHNIQUE TYPE THREE

Here, one letter is taken from the word on the left and is added to or placed into the word on the right so two new sensible words are formed. These new words must be correctly spelt. All the other letters of the words must remain in the same order as they were.

Example:

> L E A P and B A T become (_____) and (_____)

Technique:

1. Lay your pencil flat on this page and move it so that the point covers the first letter of L E A P.

   Now you read E A P.

2. Ask yourself: Does this make a sensible word?

3. If the answer is 'no', move your pencil to cover the next letter only - the E.

   Now you can see L A P.

4. Does this make a sensible word?

5. If it does not, continue with the procedure moving your pencil along, covering one letter at a time, until you can find a letter you can remove and still be left with a sensible word.

6. If the word you have now does make sense (and here it does, you are left with L A P), mentally move the *E* over to the second word. You must now add it to, or place it into, the word B A T to make another new sensible word.

7. PLACE IT IN FRONT OF THE WORD FIRST.
   This is very important and is often overlooked.

   Now you have <u>*E*</u> B A T

8. Does that make a sensible word?

9. Continue moving the *E* through the word, jumping one letter at a time, until you find a new sensible word.
   Here, jump the B and place.it between the B and the A.

10.   Does it make a sensible word?

11.   Yes. B_E_A T.

              Your two new words are: (L A P) and (B *E* A T)

NOTE:
It is not always the first letter you find to remove which is the correct one.
Here, for example:

             L E A R N and C A T become (_____) and (_____)

When the *L* is covered up, you are left with a sensible word E A R N. When you move over the *L* and test it in each position:

               L C A T   C *L* A T   C A *L* T   C A T *L*

no sensible word is formed.

So *L* IS NOT THE CORRECT LETTER TO REMOVE.
PUT IT BACK AND TRY ANOTHER.

By testing each letter, you will find you can remove the letter *R*. Now you are left with L E A N .

Add the *R* to C A T and you have:

               R C A T   C *R* A T   C A *R* T   C A T *R*

Here, the word C A *R* T is sensible.

        So, the correct answer here is (L E A N) and (C A *R* T).

You are allowed 30 seconds per question.

Now turn to the next page for Practice of this Type.

PRACTICE TYPE THREE

One letter from the word on the left-hand side must be taken and placed into or added to the word on the right-hand side so that TWO new and proper words are formed which are correctly spelt. All the other letters of the words must remain in the same position.

For Example:

L E A *R* N and C A T become (__*LEAN*__) and (__*CART*__)

Now try these:

C O U L D	and	B O N D	become	(_____)	and (_____)
C L O U D	and	P A T H	become	(_____)	and (_____)
S I G H T	and	C U E	become	(_____)	and (_____)
P L A N T	and	R A M P	become	(_____)	and (_____)
O P E N	and	S H U T	become	(_____)	and (_____)
B O A T	and	B U T	become	(_____)	and (_____)
S O A P	and	P E N	become	(_____)	and (_____)
L O N G	and	M O T H	become	(_____)	and (_____)
C R A M P	and	P A Y	become	(_____)	and (_____)
C H E A P	and	P I T H	become	(_____)	and (_____)
M E T A L	and	P E A L	become	(_____)	and (_____)
B R E A K	and	C A M P	become	(_____)	and (_____)
C H A I N	and	B E S T	become	(_____)	and (_____)
S O O N	and	D O U R	become	(_____)	and (_____)
T R A I N	and	P L A N	become	(_____)	and (_____)
F I R E	and	L O W E R	become	(_____)	and (_____)
G U I L T	and	P O N D	become	(_____)	and (_____)
C L O C K	and	H I P	become	(_____)	and (_____)
P A I N T	and	R A M	become	(_____)	and (_____)
B L I N D	and	S A Y	become	(_____)	and (_____)

TECHNIQUE TYPE FOUR

Here there are two sets of words given. You must identify one word from the left-hand set which can be joined with one word from the right-hand set to make a new sensible compound word. The word from the left-hand set must always begin the new word. You are required to underline these two 'parts'.

Example:

wall / floor / man   :   on / paper / set

Technique:

Consider each word on the left-hand side SEPARATELY with each word on the right-hand side:

1.   Test the first word on the left-hand side with each of the words on the right-hand side.

wall - on, *wall* - paper, *wall* - set

2.   Continue then onto the second word on the left-hand side. Test that with each of the three words on the right-hand side.

floor - on, *floor* - paper, *floor* - set

3.   Finally, test the third word on the left-hand side with each of the words on the right-hand side.

man - on, *man* - paper, *man* - set

(Here, the answer is *wallpaper*.)

NOTE:

1. By following the above technique, no possible combination will be overlooked as you are applying a thorough and systematic method. DO NOT 'jump about' looking randomly for the new word. This will often result in a waste of valuable time.

2. The new word often DOES NOT sound like the two separate words which you have chosen.

Example:

so	-	lid	=	solid
fat	-	her	=	father
met	-	hod	=	method
is	-	land	=	island
he	-	at	=	heat

To overcome this it is a matter of trying to 'slur' the pronunciation of the two words as you say them to yourself, if they do not appear to you on the first 'run through'. Be aware of letter combinations such as t - h, s - h, c - h, e - e, e - a and remember letters often blend to form a completely new and different sound.

3. The new word created must be a complete word in its own right such as 'playground', 'fireplace', 'wallpaper' and 'football'. It must not be a 'new' word which although it may have a new meaning, still remains as two separate words, such as 'wedding day', 'car park', 'window frame' and 'sofa bed'. These combinations are often put in to 'catch you out'!

Example:

> *pl__ay__* / wind / set   :   low / *ground* / up

Even though here *play* can be linked with 'ground' and 'up', *playground* is the correct answer as 'play up' remains as two separate words.

You are allowed 30 seconds per question.

Now turn to the next page for Practice of this Type.

PRACTICE TYPE FOUR

A word on the left-hand side will join together with a word on the right-hand side to form a completely new and proper word. The word on the left-hand side always begins this new word. Underline the two words, one from each group.

For Example:

sit / will / *man* : now / *age* / ton

Now try these:

box / police / hit   :   post / station / man

ten / he / up   :   on / so / hat

lace / hop / sat   :   near / up / in

post / cut / win   :   she / man / big

hear / wit / book   :   cat / ear / her

sofa / deck / ship   :   lay / bed / chair

go / house / from   :   pond / wife / roof

be / pal / pup   :   will / at / on

met / top / me   :   ten / in / an

hot / hay / pin   :   cup / stack / win

lost / mess / cross   :   age / ace / ice

will / in / near   :   on / by / sit

toe / hang / foot   :   shoe / ball / on

cat / lid / no   :   up / in / on

rim / rat / set   :   hot / him / her

tin / stamp / letter   :   post / box / opener

slit / met / cup   :   her / ton / man

bus / car / way   :   gone / goes / give

well / block / cat   :   age / cup / hat

sit / lamp / bath   :   chair / room / way

TECHNIQUE TYPE FIVE

These are very simple, fun to do and easy marks!

Here, a FOUR-letter word is hidden between two adjacent words. You must identify this four-letter word and write it separately in the brackets given.

(The word usually has FOUR letters in it, but BE SURE ALWAYS to read the instructions at the top of the exercise so you know precisely what you are looking for.)

Technique:

1. USING YOUR THUMBS, place them so that only FOUR letters between two words can be seen. These are the usual combinations of letters you must consider:

3 letters	-	gap	-	1 letter
2 letters	-	gap	-	2 letters
1 letter	-	gap	-	3 letters

    Remember there is ALWAYS a gap amongst the letters as you are looking for four letters hidden BETWEEN words.

2. Slowly move your thumbs along the sentence and eventually a four-letter word will be found.

    DO NOT panic if you have not found it and you are near to the end of the sentence. You will always find it if you take care.

Now try these examples:

I ha*te am*ber . . . . (___*team*___)

Combinations of letters you should look at:

a.	THUMB) I hat (THUMB	Is this a sensible word? No
b.	· THUMB) ate a (THUMB	Is this a sensible word? No
c.	THUMB) te am (THUMB	Is this a sensible word? Yes.

She ran *so fa*st she fell. . . . .(___*sofa*___)

Combinations of letters you should look at:

        a.   she r
        b.   he ra
        c.   e ran
        d.   ran s
        e.   an so
        f.   n so f
        g.   *so fa* ✓

You are allowed 30 seconds per question.

Now turn to the next page for Practice of this Type.

PRACTICE TYPE FIVE

Find the FOUR-letter word which is hidden in each of the following sentences. Each four-letter word can be found by studying the letters at the end of one word and the letters at the beginning of the next word. Write this word in the brackets.

For Example :

He has los*t his* dog . . . . (__*this*__)

Now try these:

Scientific papers and books . . . . (_____)

Most operations are successful . . . . (_____)

They looked but all they found was air . . . . (_____)

Don't enter the library . . . . (_____)

She runs tepid water . . . . (_____)

She ran so fast she fell . . . . (_____)

She came in and fell over a cat . . . . (_____)

On a dark road one must take care . . . . (_____)

Are you sure one street lamp is enough ? . . . . (_____)

He came with his sister . . . . (_____)

She was cooking with a blend of spices . . . . (_____)

He was wounded in the accident . . . . (_____)

Close the window near the door . . . . (_____)

You are tired so rest a while . . . . (_____)

The footballer was quick on the attack . . . . (_____)

They pushed her over . . . . (_____)

Hand me the material . . . . (_____)

He is so high and mighty . . . . (_____)

Do not expect too much . . . . (_____)

Quickly enter my room . . . . (_____)

TECHNIQUE TYPE SIX

Children have been enjoying this type of verbal reasoning question as quizzes in fun-books since they were toddlers. Changing one word into another in two stages.

Here two words are given. The child must calculate the word which will come in between, so one word is changed logically into another word in 2 steps, that is by changing only 1 letter each stage.

Example :

Write the word which will come in the middle :

B E A T

_____

R E A D

Technique :

1. Study both words and calculate which letters change and which do not change. Write the letters which remain unchanged in the spaces provided.

    Here E and A remain unchanged.
    Write in *E* and *A* .

B E A T

_ *E A* _

R E A D

2. Now you may change only one of the remaining letters at a time. Here B needs to be changed to R , and T to D.

3. Decide which letter to change first (Stage 1).

    For instance:

    If the B is changed to R first, then T must remain unchanged as we can only change one letter at a time.

So we have:

B E A T

R E A T

If the T is changed to D first, the B must remain unchanged. So we have:

B E A T

B E A *D*

4.   Which of these two words is a proper word ?

R E A T or B E A D ?

Only one of these words will be correct. Here *B E A D* is correct.

The B will be changed to *R* in Stage 2.

The correct answer then is :

B E A T

B E A D   Stage 1

Stage 2   R E A D

You are allowed 30 seconds per question.

Now turn to the next page for Practice of this Type.

PRACTICE TYPE SIX

In each of the following questions you must change one letter in the top word to make a new sensible word. By changing a different letter of this new word it is possible to make the bottom word, which is given. Write out the sensible word on the line provided.

For Example:

ROAD
————   becomes
FOAM

ROAD
ROAM
FOAM

~~~~~~

BORN	FIRM	PLAN	TOOL
————	————	————	————
SORE	HARM	PLOY	BOIL

~~~~~~

FALL	TREE	BOOK	HEAT
————	————	————	————
SAIL	FRET	CORK	HEMP

~~~~~~

TASK	HIVE	LASS	WEED
————	————	————	————
WALK	CAVE	FAST	WELL

~~~~~~

ROOF	BELL	FARE	STEW
————	————	————	————
HOOP	BALK	BARK	FLEW

~~~~~~

CALM	FLIP	FIST	BARK
————	————	————	————
PALE	SLIM	WISH	DART

TECHNIQUE TYPE SEVEN

Vocabulary is very important here.

You are required to find two (or more) words - one from the left-hand set of words, and one from the right-hand set of words which:

a. **have a SIMILAR meaning to each other, OR**
b. **have an OPPOSITE meaning to each other, OR (two words)**
c. **one which is SIMILAR to, and one which is OPPOSITE to another word given.**

BE SURE to read the instructions carefully so you know precisely what you are being asked to find.

> THINK — HOW MANY words am I being asked for?
>   — have they to be OPPOSITE or SIMILAR, or one of each?

Marks can be lost very easily by not reading the instructions carefully.

Often the format of these questions is similar to Type Four questions, that is, in two groups of three words. In this case, the same procedure as for Type Four must be adopted, that is testing one word at a time with all possible combinations. Let us work through an example together.

Example One:

Underline TWO words, one from each set of words, which are SIMILAR to each other in meaning:

replace / mend / avoid   :   recall / repair / shout

Technique:

1. Test: *replace* - recall, *replace* - repair, *replace* - shout

    Is there a pair of words here which are SIMILAR in meaning?
    No. Move on to the second word.

2. Test: *mend* - recall,   *mend* - repair,   *mend* - shout

    Is there a pair of words here which are SIMILAR in meaning?
    Yes.   *mend - repair*. Check (if you have time) the third word.

3. Test: *avoid* - recall,   *avoid* - repair,   *avoid* - shout

This should confirm that *mend - repair* is the only pair of words which are SIMILAR in meaning. Be sure to adopt this systematic approach and practise it so it becomes automatic. Otherwise you may miss possible correct combinations and lose marks.

The format may vary. Sometimes one word, often in capital letters, is given outside a pair of brackets. You must find one word (or more) from within the brackets which has the same (or opposite, or one similar and one opposite) meaning to this word.

The procedure is exactly the same. Test the one word outside the brackets quite separately and systematically with each word inside the brackets, until the answer is found.

Example Two:

Underline ONE word inside the brackets which is OPPOSITE in meaning to the word in capitals outside the brackets:

STRONG   (calm, tired, big, *weak*, numerous)

Technique:

Test:	a.	STRONG	-	calm
	b.	STRONG	-	tired
	c.	STRONG	-	big
	d.	STRONG	-	weak
	e.	STRONG	-	numerous

Here, STRONG and *weak* would be opposite.

NOTE:

1. If you are not certain that you have found the correct words, try placing both words, one at a time, into the same sentence, to test if the opposite (or same) meaning is conveyed.

In Example One: - *mend* and *repair*
Try: I am going to *mend* my bicycle.
          I am going to *repair* my bicycle.

Do these two sentences 'say' the SAME thing?

Similarly, in Example Two: - *STRONG* and *weak*
Try: The STRONG man lifted the heavy load.
          The *weak* man (could not) lift the heavy load.

Do these two sentences 'say' the OPPOSITE thing?

2. Encourage the use of a dictionary to look up and record the meaning of any word which is unfamiliar to your child. Suggest ways in which some of these 'new' words might be used at school this week.

You are allowed 30 seconds per question.

Now turn to the next page for Practice of this Type.

PRACTICE TYPE SEVEN

Underline TWO words in the brackets which have the SAME or nearly the same meaning as the word in capitals outside the brackets.

For Example:

ASSEMBLE (committee, *collect,* model, *gather*, kit)

Now try these:

REMEDY . . . . (hospital, patient, cure, doctor, solution)

PURCHASE . . . . (package, shop, buy, prohibit, acquire)

ODOUR . . . . (odious, occur, smell, fragrance, order)

NIMBLE . . . . (agile, stiff, aerobic, spry, weak)

ROBUST . . . . (resort, vigorous, vulnerable, strong, metal)

NECESSARY . . . . (essential, vigour, imperative, convey, frantic)

ROTATE. . . . . (ration, revolve, mower, gyrate, circumference)

Here you must underline TWO words in the brackets. One must have the SAME or nearly the same meaning as the word in capitals, the other must be OPPOSITE in meaning.

For Example:

COMMENCE (introduction, *begin*, present, *end*, over)

Now try these:

STUBBORN . . . . (horse, mule, obstinate, flexible, stain)

TRANSPARENT . . . . (glass, clear, opposite, opaque, cellophane)

TRANQUIL . . . . (peaceful, country, cottage, noisy, busy)

VACANT . . . . (flat, occupied, stare, empty, holiday)

ABANDON . . . . (quit, ship, stay, island, inhabit)

CONCEAL . . . . (surprise, hide, convey, reveal, replenish)

ENEMY . . . . (battle, friend, invade, foe, endeavour)

EXTERIOR . . . . (paint, outside, exterminate, interior, inferior)

PROHIBIT . . . . (private, allow, forbid, provide, trespass)

PECULIAR . . . . (extinct, extract, odd, usual, pedantic)

AID . . . . (hospital, assist, anxiety, obstruct, obstreperous)

DILIGENT . . . . (helpful, indolent, industrious, wary, peaceful)

COMMENCE . . . . (begin, allow, carry, attempt, conclude)

TECHNIQUE TYPE EIGHT

In this type of verbal reasoning question, you have to study each of two pairs of words to identify a rule - to discover what is happening each time to the first word in order to form the second word in each pair. You are then given the first word of a third pair. By applying the same rule as you have identified in the first two pairs, you can complete the third pair. The answer is then placed into brackets.

Example:

father, fate / matter, mate / rather, (__rate__)

Technique:

1. Ask: How has 'father' become 'fate'?
   Answer: the 1st, 2nd, 3rd and 5th letters have been used.

2. Does 'mate' come from 'matter' when I apply the same rule?
   Does the 1st, 2nd, 3rd and 5th letters of 'matter' spell 'mate'?
   If the answer is 'yes' you have found the rule.

3. Apply this rule to the third pair.
   Take the 1st, 2nd, 3rd and 5th letters of 'rather'.

1 2 3 4 5 6	1 2 3 5
r a t h e r	r a t e

   This gives the answer *rate*.

4. Check:
   Is this a reasonable answer? Is *rate* a sensible word?

Here is another Example:

Complete the third pair of words:

tears, star / pains, spin / trays, (__stay__)

Technique:

1. Give a number to each letter of the first word in the first pair of words.

1 2 3 4 5	5 1 3 4
t e a r s	s t a r

2. Calculate the 'code' for the second word using these numbers.

3.   Repeat Point 1 above for the first word of the second pair of words.

1 2 3 4 5   5 1 3 4
p a i n s   *s p i n*

4.   Test the 'code' you have calculated on the second word of this pair. Does your code 'fit' the word you are given?

5.   If the answer is 'yes' use the code to find the missing word in the third pair of words.

1 2 3 4 5   5 1 3 4
t r a y s   *s t a y*

NOTE:

1. Sometimes the first letter only may change, perhaps to the next letter in the alphabet. For example:

*b*oast, *c*oast / *g*ear, *h*ear / *m*eat, (_neat_)

2. Sometimes two letters may change, each time to the same two letters:

me*sh*, me*ss* / le*an*, le*ss* / mo*st*, (_moss_)

Here, the 3rd and 4th letters are changing each time to *ss*.

3. Sometimes a letter is missed off the end and another letter changed in the word:

si*ng*, su*ng* / ri*ng*, ru*ng* / swi*ng*, (_swung_)

4. Occasionally a word is spelt backwards:

golf, flog   / time, emit / doom, (_mood_)

Whatever is happening, if you apply and practise the method of numbering each letter of the first word in each pair so that it is possible to identify a pattern and hence a code, it should be possible to complete the third pair each time.

You are allowed 30 seconds per question.

Now turn to the next page for Practice of this Type.

PRACTICE TYPE EIGHT

Fill in the missing word in brackets needed to complete the third pair of words. This pair follows the same pattern as the first two pairs of words.

For Example:

    stone   tone   /   slate   late   /   cream (*_ream_*)

Now try these:

meal lame	/	teal late	/	zeal	(_____)
mast mash	/	last lash	/	cast	(_____)
live evil	/	bats stab	/	step	(_____)
stings stung	/	flings flung	/	sings	(_____)
meat mat	/	feed fed	/	seat	(_____)
medal meal	/	cream cram	/	stair	(_____)
mate tame	/	male lame	/	rapt	(_____)
but cut	/	sip tip	/	rat	(_____)
thin win	/	star war	/	soon	(_____)
save vase	/	rote tore	/	mane	(_____)
swing win	/	pales ale	/	parts	(_____)
lead deal	/	tart tart	/	nail	(_____)
oils soil	/	oaks soak	/	eats	(_____)
star rats	/	trap part	/	parts	(_____)
stagger stank	/	swagger swank	/	dagger	(_____)
rang sang	/	same tame	/	balm	(_____)
late tale	/	tame mate	/	mace	(_____)
car race	/	man name	/	but	(_____)
stare tart	/	spare part	/	scare	(_____)
lamp palm	/	pier ripe	/	tier	(_____)

TECHNIQUE TYPE NINE

These are simple crossword exercises.

A grid three letters wide and three letters deep is given with one word already written into it. Five more words are listed on the outside of the grid. You are asked to fit these five words into the grid to complete the 'crossword'.

Example:

			POT
			TEN
			PIP
			ORE
P	E	N	IRE

Technique:

1. Study the five words listed outside the grid. You must choose to place first the one word which can fit into one position only. For instance, in the above example, there is one word only that ends in *P*. The only word therefore that could be placed in the first column down is *PIP*. There is no choice about this. Similarly, I could place *TEN*. *TEN* is the only word which ends in *N*. *TEN* could therefore be placed in the third column down. Again there is no choice about this. I have, however, two words which end in *E - IRE* and *ORE*. Either of these words could be placed in the middle column down. Since I do not know which one would be correct, this would not be a good place to start.
   PLACE FIRST THE WORD WHICH CAN FIT INTO ONE POSITION ONLY.

2. If I place *PIP*, therefore, into the first column down, I can then see that the first word across the top line must also begin with a *P*. The only word that could go into this position then, would be *POT* as this is the only word which begins with *P*. I enter *POT*.

P	O	T	POT
I			TEN
P	E	N	PIP
			ORE
			IRE

3. It is now obvious that *TEN* must be placed in the third column down, and *R* in the very centre of the grid. The *R* will give *IRE* across and *ORE* down. The 'crossword' is now complete.

Answer:

P	*O*	*T*
I	*R*	*E*
P	*E*	*N*

This exercise must be completed in 30 seconds.

Example:

M	A	N	ODE
			NET
			DOT
			ADO
			MOD

Technique:

1.   Here,   *MOD* is the only word beginning with *M*
                              ADO is the only word beginning with *A*
                              NET is the only word beginning with *N*
so there is quite a choice of first words to put into the grid. I shall place
ADO. Once *ADO* has been placed, I stop and study the remaining words,
looking for a word that will now fit.

M	A	N	ODE
	D		NET
	O		DOT
			ADO
			MOD

2.   It is obvious now that *MOD* must be placed in the first column down, and
      NET in the third column down. On checking I can see that *DOT* and *ODE*
      have been created automatically by the position of the other letters. The grid
      is now complete.

Answer:

M	*A*	*N*
O	*D*	*E*
D	*O*	*T*

You are allowed 30 seconds per question.

Now turn to the next page for Practice of this Type.

PRACTICE TYPE NINE

The following are a type of simple crossword. Complete each puzzle by fitting the five words on the right-hand side of the grid horizontally or vertically into the correct positions. One word has already been included.

For Example:

A	P	E

SAM
MEN
TEN
APE
SAT

becomes

S	*A*	*M*
A	*P*	*E*
T	*E*	*N*

Now try these:

S	O	N

ASP
END
TOO
POD
ATE

	O	
	D	
	E	

WAS
SET
NOT
ADO
WON

		W
		R
		Y

EAR
TRY
OAR
LOW
LET

S	A	T

AGO
TEN
WON
SAW
AGE

M		
E		
T		

TON
TEN
AGE
MAT
EGO

E	Y	E

COY
ACT
TEE
ATE
TOE

O	N	E

EWE
ORE
EVE
REV
NEW

P		
A		
R		

ARE
IRE
RED
PIT
TED

		T
		E
		D

END
ONE
WOE
INN
WIT

A	T	E

TOE
TEE
EWE
NOW
ANT

TECHNIQUE TYPE TEN

Here you are given a set of words, often in capital letters, outside a pair of brackets, and more words inside the brackets. You are asked to underline a word inside the brackets which belongs to the same family as the words outside the brackets.

Take care to read the instructions properly. Sometimes you are asked for ONE word, sometimes for TWO words which are connected in the same way.

Example:

OAK   ASH   SYCAMORE (branch, leaf, daffodil, elm, garden)

Technique:

1.   Do not consider the words inside the brackets until you have studied the words outside the brackets. Look only at these words and decide what connection there is between them. Here, for instance, concentrate only on the words in capital letters outside the brackets: OAK, ASH, SYCAMORE. Ask: What is the connection between oak, ash and sycamore?

Answer: They are all types of tree.

2.   You should now have this in the front of your mind when you look at the words inside the brackets. You are looking for a TYPE of tree.
The NAME of a tree - not a part of a tree.

Here, elm is the answer.

Example:

SWALLOW   ROBIN   WREN (nest, feather, chirp, thrush, food)

1.   Ask: What is the connection between SWALLOW, ROBIN and WREN?

Answer: They are all types of bird.

2.   Go into the brackets now, already knowing that you are looking for a TYPE of bird. Do not be distracted by words closely related to 'bird'.

Here, the answer is thrush.

You are allowed 30 seconds per question.

Now turn to the next page for Practice of this Type.

PRACTICE TYPE TEN

There is a connection between the three words on the outside of the brackets and TWO of the words inside the brackets. Underline the TWO words.

For Example :

ABANDON DESERT FORSAKE (island, *leave*, ship, sand, *quit*)

Now try these:

NEEDLES THREAD SCISSORS .... (pine, pins, cramp, thimble, cut)

PENCIL PEN CHARCOAL .... (chalk, ink, crayon, ruler, colour)

PILLOW SHEET BLANKET . (bedroom, duvet, mattress, sleep, dream)

HELMET TURBAN SOMBRERO .... (head, cap, scarf, fez, motorcycle)

CUP SAUCER PLATE .... (table, napkin, beaker, bowl, spoon)

SHOULDER KNEE ELBOW ...... (body, wrist, person, ankle, sprain)

STOMACH HEART BRAIN .... (surgeon, hospital, lungs, kidney, foot)

KING PRINCE NEPHEW .... (aunt, queen, uncle, mother, boy)

QUEEN LADY MOTHER .... (king, lord, aunt, prince, princess)

OCEAN RIVER LAKE .... (pond, wave, stream, boat, rain)

KITTEN CALF FOAL .... (cat, cub, cygnet, horse, cow)

BUFFALO BEAR BEAVER .... (badger, banana, bull, bracelet, basket)

OAK ELM ASH .... (tree, leaf, sycamore, chestnut, trunk)

ANT BEE BUTTERFLY .... (midge, honey, wings, gnat, cocoon)

OIL COFFEE SOUP ...... (lubricate, paraffin, vegetable, brine, bowl)

BOOT SHOE SLIPPER .... (foot, sock, sandal, tennis, plimsolls)

BOTTLE JUG CARTON .... (keg, milk, water, flagon, wine)

SHIP BARGE KAYAK .... (sail, canoe, canal, yacht, crew)

PIANO VIOLIN CELLO .... (trumpet, harp, viola, trombone, drum)

TRUMPET TUBA FLUTE .... (piano, cornet, cymbal, saxophone, harp)

TECHNIQUE TYPE ELEVEN

In this Type of verbal reasoning question you are given several groups
of words. The words inside each group are closely related to each other,
but there is no connection between the groups. Underneath you are
given a list of words and simply asked to identify to which group each of
the words belongs.

Example:

A	B	C	D	E
spade	jumper	house	fast	lamb
hoe	trousers	flat	quick	kitten
shears	coat	villa	speedy	puppy
lawnmower	dress	bungalow	hasty	calf

Into which group would you place the following?
Write A, B, C, D or E in the brackets next to each word.

socks	(_B_)	wheelbarrow	(_A_)	hat	(_B_)
caravan	(_C_)	cygnet	(_E_)	trowel	(_A_)
gosling	(_E_)	rake	(_A_)	spry	(_D_)
foal	(_E_)	tent	(_C_)	swift	(_D_)

Technique:

1. Study each group A to E .
    Classify each group - decide what each group is.
    Here,

    A is a set of garden implements
    B is a set of clothes
    C are all types of dwelling
    D are all words meaning 'speedy'
    E is a set of young animals

2. Now work through the list of words, carefully deciding to which group each
    word belongs.

These are easy marks, and fun to do. Just take care.
One mark is awarded for each correct answer.

You are allowed 30 seconds per question.

Now turn to the next page for Practice of this Type.

PRACTICE TYPE ELEVEN

Below are five groups of words labelled A, B, C, D and E. There is a
connection between each member of each group, but there is no
connection between the groups. Below these there are twelve words.
Identify the group to which each of these words belongs. Write the
letter of the group in the brackets next to the word.

A	B	C	D	E
trumpet	cow	Mars	tulip	scarlet
tuba	horse	Jupiter	gladiolus	indigo
trombone	giraffe	Earth	lupin	violet
flute	puma	Saturn	daisy	ochre

rouge   (____)   oboe   (____)   crimson (____)

Pluto   (____)   Mercury   (____)   clarinet (____)

koala   (____)   cowslip   (____)   shrew   (____)

cornet   (____)   piccolo   (____)   taupe   (____)

A	B	C	D	E
butcher	teak	nickel	tea	earwig
draper	oak	tin	vinegar	gnat
lawyer	mahogany	zinc	water	grasshopper
plumber	beech	copper	wine	butterfly

iron   (____)   balsa   (____)   paraffin (____)

brine   (____)   mason   (____)   ant   (____)

locust   (____)   tailor   (____)   platinum (____)

pine   (____)   bronze   (____)   rowan   (____)

TECHNIQUE TYPE TWELVE

Here you are required to find the 'odd one out' of a set of items. Sometimes ONE, sometimes TWO items do not belong with the others. Sometimes ONE or TWO items are similar to each other but different from the others. You must identify them and underline your answer.

Read the instructions carefully. Make sure you know what you are being asked for. Do not lose these easy marks by being careless here.

Example:

In each of the following sets there is one word which does not belong with the other words. Underline this 'odd one out'.

(cup   plate   saucer   tureen   spoon   jug)

(hat   bag   coat   tee-shirt   skirt   jumper)

(house   flat   villa   sea   bungalow)

(car   truck   van   liner   bus)

(4   36   49   72   81) *

Technique:

1.   Systematically compare each word in the set.

    a)   Take the first word and look over all the remaining words to see if it is the same (or different to) the others in the set.

    b)   Move onto the next word and compare that word carefully with the rest.

2.   Work through the set in this way until you find the word (words) you are looking for.

3.   Underline or re-write them. . . . . . whatever you are asked to do.

NOTE:
1. * Know your square numbers.
A square number is the outcome when a number is multiplied by itself.

Example:

2 x 2 = 4   3 x 3 = 9   6 x 6 = 36

4   9   16   25   36   49   64 . . . . are square numbers.

These occur frequently on verbal reasoning test papers.

2. Use a Thesaurus to familiarise yourself with synonyms - enjoy finding words of similar meaning. Ask a parent to set you perhaps five words a week to look up in a Thesaurus. Words such as wily, tepid, defy, dissent, remiss, amass. Try to extend your vocabulary so you can quickly recognise a word which is an 'odd one out' in a list of words. This exercise will also help to improve your performance in Type Seven.

Example:

Identify the TWO words which are similar to each other but different from the rest :

(round   heavy   lead   glass   square)

Using the above Technique, compare:

round - heavy,   *round* - lead,   *round* - glass,   *round* - square

heavy - lead,   *heavy* - glass,   *heavy* - square

lead - glass,   *lead* - square

glass - square

Answer: *round - square*

Now try these:

	Answers:
(swing grass slide house child)	*swing - slide*
(book cat fireplace nut magazine)	*book - magazine*
(sock pencil church rest chalk)	*pencil - chalk*
(clock plant curtain hat watch)	*clock - watch*

Answers to Example overleaf:

spoon   bag   sea   liner   72

You are allowed 30 seconds per question.

Now turn to the next page for Practice of this Type.

PRACTICE TYPE TWELVE

Each of the following sets of brackets has ONE word which does NOT belong to the rest. Underline this 'odd one out'.

For Example:

(cap   helmet   *head*   sombrero   turban)

Now try these:

(hedgehog   mole   badger   sparrow   mouse)

(retreiver   greyhound   dogfish   collie   spaniel)

(chaffinch   duck   goose   mongoose   eagle)

(cod   eel   herring   mackerel   heron)

(racket   golf   rugby   football   hockey)

(gladiolus   iris   lilac   lily   petal)

(cone   chestnut   beech   larch   oak)

(orange   apple   banana   pip   pear)

(lettuce   tomato   cucumber   mayonnaise   raddish)

(lead   metal   iron   zinc   copper)

(milk   lemonade   bottle   oil   paraffin)

(beak   nest   feather   wing   talon)

(diamond   emerald   pearl   topaz   ruby)

(queen   prince   lord   man   king)

(lord   aunt   mother   lady   sister)

(plate   cup   beaker   saucer   fork)

(wheat   oats   cereal   barley   maize)

(runs   bounds   athlete   jogs   gallops)

(purrs   cat   growls   neighs   brays)

(Canada   Whales   Scotland   England   France)

TECHNIQUE TYPE THIRTEEN

Here you are simply asked to put items in order of size, sequence or position.

Be careful! These questions are simple but it is very easy to lose marks through carelessness. Are you asked to order them SMALLEST first, LARGEST first or for an item in a specific position, for instance in the MIDDLE ? Read the instructions carefully.

If you are asked for an item in the MIDDLE, you will be given an odd number of items (either 5 or 7). To work out which will be the middle of a set of 5 items it is not necessary to rank all the items 1 to 5 to get an answer, only 1 to 3. It is then the 3rd item you need. In a list of 7 items it is the 4th item you need and so on. Being aware of these small points will help to save time in an examination.

Things you are often asked about in this Type of question:

1. SHAPES - know your shapes. How many sides has a triangle, rectangle, pentagon, hexagon, octogon and so on?

2. TIME - as well as knowing the units of time - second, minute, hour, day, week, month, year and so on - know also how to read time in terms of the 24 hour clock, digital time and also 'o'clock'.

3. MONTHS of the year - know them in order. Similarly,

4. DAYS of the week. Know that day one is always Sunday.

5. Know such things as the ranking of soldiers - private, corporal, sergeant, lieutenant, major, colonel, and so on.

6. Have some idea about the size of different boats - canoe, kayak, ocean liners, a tug, dinghy and so on.

7. Metric units - know the order in which they come - millimetre, centimetre, metre, kilometre; millilitre, litre; gram, kilogram.

8. Know what a HAMLET is. Know what an EMBRYO is.

9. Know the difference between a syllable, sentence, paragraph and so on.

10. Know expressions such as solo, duet, trio, quartet, quintet, sextet and so on.

You are allowed 30 seconds per question.

Now turn to the next page for Practice of this Type.

PRACTICE TYPE THIRTEEN

Underline the word that would come in the MIDDLE if the following were put in order of size, sequence or position.

For Example:

(football   golf ball   *tennis ball*   volley ball   marble)

Now try these:

(truck   bicycle   motorbike   car   van)

(28   36   14   88   49)

(orange   melon   grape   plum   grapefruit)

(sergeant   colonel   corporal   major   private)

(baby   youth   embryo   adult   toddler)

(thimble   jug   mug   cup   eggcup)

(2 a.m.   18.30   00.30   3. 15 a.m.   7.30 p.m.)

(March   January   September   July   November)

(second   hour   minute   day   week)

(pentagon   triangle   octogon   rectangle   hexagon)

(£4.40   £44.00   £4.04   £14.44   £0.40)

(tug   liner   kayak   canoe   aircraft carrier)

(Friday   Tuesday   Thursday   Wednesday   Monday)

(163   631   361   663   366)

(ninth   sixteenth   first   fifth   third)

(horse   sheep   cat   dog   mouse)

(letter   syllable   paragraph   word   sentence)

(estuary   river   sea   source   brook)

(handbag   purse   shopping bag   suitcase   trunk)

(quintet   solo   quartet   trio   duet)

PRIZE CERTIFICATE

Pupil's Name: ....

This is to certify that the above-named pupil has completed the Practice Exercises in Verbal Reasoning Technique and Practice 1 and has achieved

a BEST SCORE of .... within the time allowed.

I .... (Parent)

am extremely proud of these achievements and undertake to

(insert details of Special Award) ....

....

in recognition of this achievement and to show my appreciation of all the hard work and effort that has gone into doing so well.

Well Done!
Congratulations!

ADDITIONAL EXERCISES

Additional exercises to improve your child's speed and accuracy.

A.   **To improve ability to listen to instructions and carry them out quickly and accurately.**

Take any story book, and ask your child to find certain things in it, for instance:

a.   What is the third word on the fourth line on page 15?

b.   How many letters are in the last word on the bottom of page 16?

c.   How many vowels are there in the seventh word on the fourteenth line of page 10?

d.   How many a's are there in the sixth word on the ninth line on page 7, and so on.

B.   **To improve your child's ability to work through the alphabet quickly and accurately.**

Take a dictionary and ask your child to open the page at the letter 'M', 'N', 'B' and so on, so he learns to judge the position of the letters in the alphabet and is able to estimate where to open the dictionary to find a particular letter.

C.   **To give your child a concept of 30 seconds and so be able to pace himself in an examination that requires him to answer one question in 30 seconds.**

a.   While checking with your own watch ask your child to tell you when he thinks 30 seconds has passed. Repeat until he can judge it accurately within 5 seconds either side.

b.   'Speed handwriting' - see how many times he can write his name in 30 seconds. Try again. Can he improve his 'record'? Many children I have taught can achieve up to 30 five-letter words in 30 seconds!

TRY TO AWAKEN YOUR CHILD'S INNATE SPEED
WHILE MAINTAINING ACCURACY.

PERSONAL RECORD TABLE

Name: . . . .

DATE	TYPE	No.of Qs	SCORE	MAX. TIME	ACTUAL TIME	COMMENTS
	1	20		10		
	2	20		10		
	3	20		10		
	4	20		10		
	5	20		10		
	6	20		10		
	7	20		10		
	8	20		10		
	9	10		5		
	10	20		10		
	11	24		12		
	12	20		10		
	13	20		10		

How to fill in the PERSONAL RECORD TABLE:

The parent should fill in the Date of the test in Column 1.
What is your child's score? Enter in Column 4.
Enter your child's Actual Time in Column 6.
Do you need to make a note of anything?
Could your child do with more practice ?
Was his score high enough?
There are more Practice Exercises of all these Types in Verbal Reasoning Further Practice Exercises.
What about your child's time? Is that: Good?   Bad?   Getting better?
Record your Comments in Column 7.

ANSWERS

TYPE ONE:

the (2nd), ball
to, his
across, into
the, quickly
up, down
hot, cold
in, out
it, into
is, milk
slippers, table
be, quiet
no, deck
church, in
shoes, cloakroom
nine, seven
Friday, Sunday
in, out
at, herself
come, in
fir, bend

TYPE TWO:

road, canal
head, glove
ring, bracelet
mood, moor
heat, light
yellow, red
live, time
root, foundations
trick, prick
book, composer
10, 25 (+5!)
metre, millilitre
cart, part
hot, cold
apple, potato
lead, ink
pentagon, rectangle
look, listen
steam, gas
write, paint

TYPE THREE:

COLD, BOUND
LOUD, PATCH
SIGH, CUTE
PLAN, TRAMP
PEN, SHOUT
BAT, BOUT
SAP, OPEN
LOG, MONTH
CAMP, PRAY
HEAP, PITCH
MEAL, PETAL
BEAK, CRAMP
CHIN, BEAST
SON, ODOUR
RAIN, PLANT
IRE, FLOWER
GILT, POUND
LOCK, CHIP
PAIN, TRAM
BIND, SLAY

TYPE FOUR:

policeman
upon
satin
postman
wither
deckchair
housewife
beat
mean
haystack
message
nearby
football
noon
rather
letterbox
slither
cargoes
blockage
bathroom

TYPE FIVE:

sand
stop
tall
tent
step
sofa
love
done
nest
hiss
able
dint
down
sore
heat
hero
them
hand
note
term

TYPE SIX:

BORE
FARM
PLAY
TOIL
FAIL
FREE
COOK
HEAP
TALK
HAVE
LAST
WELD
HOOF
BALL
BARE
SLEW
PALM
SLIP
FISH
DARK

TYPE SEVEN:

cure solution
buy acquire
smell fragrance
agile spry
strong vigorous
imperative essential
revolve gyrate
obstinate flexible
clear opaque
peaceful noisy
occupied empty
quit stay
hide reveal
friend foe
outside interior
allow forbid
odd usual
assist obstruct
indolent industrious
begin conclude

TYPE EIGHT:

laze
cash
pets
sung
sat
stir
part
sat
won
name
art
lain
seat
strap
dank
calm
came
tube
cart
rite

TYPE NINE:

ATE	SON
WON	ADO
LOW	EAR
SAT	AGE
MAT	EGO
ACT	TOE
ONE	REV
PIT	ARE
WIT	ONE
ATE	NOW

POD	SET
TRY	WON
TEN	EYE
EWE	RED
END	TEE

TYPE TEN:

thimble pins
chalk crayon
duvet mattress
cap fez
beaker bowl
wrist ankle
lungs kidney
uncle boy
aunt princess
pond stream
cub cygnet
badger bull
sycamore chestnut
midge gnat
paraffin brine
sandal plimsolls
keg flagon
canoe yacht
harp viola
cornet saxophone

ANSWERS

TYPE ELEVEN:

E	A	E
C	C	A
B	D	B
A	A	E
C	B	D
D	A	E
E		C
B		B

TYPE TWELVE:

- sparrow
- dogfish
- mongoose
- heron
- racket
- petal
- cone
- pip
- mayonnaise
- metal
- bottle
- nest
- pearl
- queen
- lord
- fork
- cereal
- athlete
- cat
- whales

TYPE THIRTEEN:

- car
- 36
- orange
- sergeant
- toddler
- cup
- 3.15 a.m.
- July
- hour
- pentagon
- £4.40
- tug
- Wednesday
- 366
- fifth
- dog
- word
- river
- shopping bag
- trio